Oh Brother, My Brother

Two Brothers. Blended Family. A Journey of Healing.

Brandon D. Campbell

HOHM PRESS
Chino Valley, AZ

Cover design: Hohm Press
Interior design and layout by Becky Fulker, Kubera Book Design
Illustration Credits: Shanzay Saquib

Print ISBN: 978-1-963433-12-8
eBook ISBN: 978-1-963433-13-5

Library of Congress Control Number: Applied for.

Printed and bound in China
First printing: February 2026

Hohm Press
P.O. Box 4410
Chino Valley, AZ 86323
(800) 381-2700
hohmpress.com

TABLE OF CONTENTS

DEDICATION

I dedicate this book to my brothers — Chris, Don Jr., and Kelin (who is no longer with us). You've each influenced who I am and who I am becoming, and I'm grateful for the lessons, laughter, and love that come with being part of our "perfectly imperfect" blended family.

To the men and boys searching for their place in this modern world: you are not alone. May the story of *Oh Brother, My Brother* remind you that your journey matters, your voice matters, and that with self-care, love, and connection, you can find your way.

Most of all, I dedicate this work to my beautiful wife Connie and to our three precious daughters. You're my inspiration and reason for hope. Your encouragement carried me through every page of this book. I love you.

INSTRUCTIONS FOR CONVERSATION QUESTIONS

The goal of this story is to help bring families closer. By talking and listening more, it will help you understand why things in your family are the way that they are. This may provide information to help you understand who you are and how much you're loved by your parent(s) and build your confidence.

At the end of each chapter, you'll see **Conversation Questions** for you and your parent(s) to talk about. These questions are to help you share thoughts, feelings, and ideas with each other. You can read this book together, or each of you can read it on your own and then talk about the questions afterward. If you have two parents who don't live in the same home, you can read this book with them at different times.

Why These Questions Matter

- They help you understand each other better.
- They give you a chance to discuss your thoughts.
- They're a way for you to feel closer to your parent(s).

How to Get the Most Out of These Conversations

- **Take Turns:** First, you answer a question. Then, your parents do.
- **Be Honest:** There are no wrong answers. Say how you really feel or think.
- **Listen Carefully:** When it's the other person's turn, listen to their answer without interrupting.
- **Have Fun:** It's okay to laugh or share stories while you talk!

How to Use This Book

1. **Read Together:** Sit down and take turns reading the chapters out loud. Then, answer the questions as a team.
2. **Read Separately:** You and your parent(s) can read the book on your own time. When you're ready, talk about the questions together.

Talking about these questions is a fantastic way for you to learn more about your parent(s) and for your parent(s) to learn more about you. Enjoy "Oh Brother, My Brother."

— Chapter 1 —

We're Brothers (Ohmar)

I lie still, eyes wide open, staring at the ceiling. I blink and stare some more, questions running through my mind, "Who am I? How did I get here?" I blink again. Nothing has changed. I am still in this same house, stuck with the same family.

Oh, hey there! Good morning. I am Ohmar. Only my close friends and relatives can call me "Oh," so you better not. I am a ten-year-old fourth grader. Most kids my age are in the fifth grade, but for some reason the school said that I was born late, so I had to wait an entire year to begin kindergarten. How can a kid be born late? What does that even mean? Isn't that a load of crap?

Anyway, it's Saturday, my favorite day of the week. There's no school, no chores, and did I mention no school? Oh, how I love Saturday! I'm free to do what I want when I want to do it! So, whether I'm playing football or basketball or watching football or basketball or eating oatmeal cream pies and hot potato chips and washing them down with an iced cold grape pop as I sit on the couch while watching the games, I get to have fun all day long!

But this Saturday is not like any regular Saturday. If you ask anyone in my family, it's a special Saturday because it's my little brother's seventh birthday, and we have a whole weekend of activities planned out. Please help me, God!

My little brother is Mychael, "My" for short. He's up out of bed before me, doing his usual weekend routine of playing alone with his makeshift toys. I'll admit that sometimes I rip the limbs off his figurines to see if I can put them back together again. I usually fail, but it doesn't stop me from trying. When he doesn't have toys because I break them or our usual experiment of having them sink or swim in the toilet goes wrong, Mychael uses his big imagination to create his own toys out of clothespins, wire hangers, or just about anything he can find to fit his gaming purposes!

Get this. He draws all over the white walls without getting punished. If it were me, I'd be grounded until infinity, but not Mychael. He's Mom's favorite.

I forgot to mention that Mychael and I are half-brothers. Same mom, but different dads and different last names! Mine is Bowman; his is Johnson. It's kind of embarrassing trying to explain to kids at school how we are brothers who ended up with different names—like I know how it happened. It just did, okay? In this house, you better never let my mom hear you say half-brothers. It's just brothers. We get along most of the time, but…I don't know how to describe it. We have some things in common, but we are soooo different. You'll see.

On this particular day, he's playing war super loud, waking me up with his squishy-squishing explosion noises, splashing me with the slimy spit and drool he sprays out of his mouth!

"KABOOM! Skeeeeeh! Swoosh! Boooooooooooqe! I will save you!"

"Mychael! Not again, Bro! Come on, man! You woke me up right in the middle of a good dream. I was the starting quarterback in the Pro Football Championship game. My team was down by five points, but I dropped back, escaped these big, ugly defenders, and threw a hundred-yard pass across the middle to the end zone!"

"Oh wow…Then what happened?" Mychael says with starry eyes as bright as the Big Dipper.

"Then, I woke up cause you were being so loud."

"Oh. Since you are already up...can you play with me?"

CONVERSATION QUESTIONS:

Child: What is on your mind right now? What do you think about the most? What do you dream about?

Parent: Explain what was on your mind and in your dreams when you were a child.

BEAN
42

— Chapter 2 —

Through My Little Eyes (Mychael)

Okay, so let me explain. Sure, I'm the little brother, and I love having fun. My brother Ohmar is so cool. He probably wouldn't tell anyone this, but on Saturdays, we used to see who could wake up first to open the new box of cereal and find the prize. Sometimes he'd cheat by changing the time of my alarm. Then, we'd play together all morning long. Sometimes we'd play make-believe.

We'd get out every single toy we'd gotten for Christmas and birthdays and play with them all. After the toys would somehow be broken or come up "missing," we'd find other stuff to play with. We'd take books, pins, buttons, pencils—you name it—and create a city! It had tall buildings and people living in the neighborhoods, and Ohmar would use stuffed animals to make a zoo. Our favorite game was cops and robbers. Ohmar was always the cop, making me the robber. I was sick and tired of being the robber. But it's okay because I got to play with my big bro! Now, all my brother does is play sports with the big boys down the street. And when he's not playing them, he's watching them all day long. Ugh! He used to be so fun.

This morning, I try to wake him up to play with me, but he won't budge. So, like all the other million Saturdays, I start playing without him. To Ohmar, I'm a little strange because I like playing alone. I have a great big ole imagination—so big that I can go from being an astronaut, or a world-saving superhero with the strength of one hundred men, to being a bird flying through the night skies. But I still want someone to play with.

Ohmar is too focused on being the next big superstar in three sports: baseball, football, and basketball. He wants to be like his favorite celebrity heroes. He believes one day he'll be so rich and famous our town will name a street after him!

"So, Ohmarion." (He hates it when I call him that.) "What do you say? Will you? Will you? Pleeeeeease..."

"No! Especially not now that you called me that awful name," he says, punching me in the shoulder and walking out of the room.

"Ouch! That hurts!" I scream after him.

All of a sudden, a smell hits my nose hard like a boxer in a fight. Not like Ohmar's horrible, stinky socks though—this smell is gooooood. Ohmar and I are in a daze, like zombies, following the smell into the kitchen.

CONVERSATION QUESTIONS:

Child: Do you feel like you're different? If so, what makes you different than your friends or siblings?

Parent: Explain the meaning of uniqueness. Tell your child what it is about him/her that makes them unique.

— Chapter 3 —

Oh Mom, My Mom (Ohmar)

Mom is cooking our favorite breakfast—apple pancakes! As we stagger into the kitchen, our mom is "shaking a groove thing," as she calls it.

"Do you know what today is… Hmmmm hmmm ananananah annannah." she sings.

Mom is in a sweet mood because it's Mychael's birthday, and he's the apple of her eye. To celebrate, she's made a stack of homemade buttermilk apple pancakes. Mychael being my little half…Oops I mean, brother…is not so bad, after all. It has its perks.

Our mother, Lucelle, is taller than most moms, and she has a smile that can light up the sun. It's kind of weird, but when she comes to my school, my friends are less rowdy, the teachers seem less mean, and I am the most liked. She has that sort of effect on people.

The best thing about her is how much she shows she loves my brother and me, though she tends to favor Mychael a little more. She works as a nurse at the local hospital. She is the hardest-working person I have ever seen. She must be the most liked and best nurse in the world because just last year, she won the Nurse of the Year award! Her prize was an all-expenses-paid trip to New York City, and she took us with her. New York is very different from our small, boring town.

We stayed in a fancy hotel in Times Square. Looking out the window, I could see all the lights and hear the noise from all the people and taxicabs passing by.

In the Big Apple, as it is called, we got to see the Statue of Liberty, eat cotton candy, popcorn, and a New-York-style hot dog from a real food truck in Central Park. We also visited the largest art museum in the United States called The Met and read books at the New York Public Library!

But the highlight was going to my first basketball game. This wasn't just any game. My favorite player in the whole wide world—the GOAT, Jeff Bean—was in town to go up against the New York Rockstars! Jeff Bean scored sixty points and hit the game-winning shot at the buzzer, making me and the crowd go cuckoo!

Okay, back to my mom. Although she's a single mother and doesn't make much money, she makes sure my brother and I have all our needs met. We are also lucky to have a grandma and grandpa—we call him Papa—who love us equally as much. Papa is my mom's stepdad. My granny and my mom's real dad divorced a long time ago, and then Grandma married Papa! That's all I know about my mom's daddy. Anyway, we go to my grandparents' house every day after school until my mom gets off work.

Saturdays are big days because even though I get to do a lot of what I want, it's also when our mom spends quality time with us. She probably doesn't want to play games with Mychael or sports with me, and she might even hate watching sports, but she does it all with us anyway so we can be together as a family.

Today, she's filled with joy. Mychael is the baby, so he tends to get a special amount of attention and all the hugs. Meanwhile, I get sore cheeks from getting them pinched.

"More pancakes, please," Mychael says.

"Okay, birthday boy, this is it. You will have to save some room for what your dad may have for you today."

We are enjoying our breakfast when the doorbell rings. *Ding. Dong. Ding. Dong.* Mom leaves the kitchen to see who it is.

CONVERSATION QUESTIONS:

Child: How do you feel about the amount of attention you receive? Who are your heroes? What do you want to be when you grow up?

Parent: Explain who your childhood heroes were and what you wanted to be when you were a kid.

— Chapter 4 —

My Dad (Mychael)

"It's your father!" Mom yells from the living room.

My dad's name is Mychael too. My mom and grandma tell me I look just like him. He's tall! Ohmar says he's the same height as Jeff Bean. My dad doesn't talk much or ever says he loves me, but he does give us a lot of things!

One Christmas, we didn't get many presents from Santa. My mom said it was because we moved out of our apartment into a new house with a backyard (and not because we hadn't been good or anything like that). My dad surprised my brother and me with an armful of presents. He told us that Santa must have made a mistake and dropped the gifts off at his house.

Sometimes I wish my dad lived with us. He's so cool and nice to me, my brother, and my mom. I wonder how things would be if he did. The good thing is he does come over all the time, so it doesn't make me too sad. But I hope I am not the reason he doesn't stay.

Ohmar's Point of View

"Hey, hey! Are you ready to go have some fun?" Big Mychael asks.

"Yes! I know I am," Little Mychael says.

"Me too!" I say. We race to our room to change out of our pj's and into some presentable clothes.

Moments later, we're at the Asher Boys & Girls Club, a ritzy community center on the West Side. Little Mychael is greeted by his cousins, grandpa, and aunties on his dad's side, all there to celebrate his birthday with lots of gifts in their hands. Mychael has never met his dad's mom before. Maybe his grandpa and grandmother got a divorce like our mom's dad and grandma did.

Although I'm happy for my baby bro, I can't help but compare the differences between his life and mine. I have never met my grandpa, grandma, aunts, uncles, or cousins on my dad's side of the family. I don't know anything about them, not even their names.

After the birthday cake, Mychael opens all his gifts. He plays basketball with his entire family. Even his grandpa and aunts are playing. I'm watching from a bench. I know Mychael doesn't like sports, and he really doesn't know how to play the game. He's committing every violation that was ever invented in the sport. But at one point, his grandpa, who must be a million years old, hits a three-point shot over Big Mychael's outstretched arms! I can see Mychael is having lots of fun.

I'm feeling pretty lonely on the bench. But it isn't my family, so I guess I just have to sit and watch. Then, the ball suddenly bounces out of bounds towards me. Automatically, I pick up the ball, take a few dribbles, and take a shot.

"Swoosh!"

Everyone cheers.

"I have a bright idea!" shouts Mychael.

"What's that?" Big Mychael asks.

"How about my brother and I play on the same team? We are the smallest out here, so two of us equals one of you!"

"He does make a compelling point," says Big Mychael.

So I join forces with Mychael on the same team, and we win the next two out of three games. Mychael is super happy.

"I'm glad you are my big brother," he says.

"You're my favorite little brother," I reply with a grin.

On the way home, Big Mychael takes me and Mychael to get some ice cream from our favorite place, the Pink Queen. I have the mint chocolate chip waffle cone while Mychael gets the king-size cup with a chocolate and strawberry swirl. I must say, today isn't so bad! Another good thing about being Mychael's big bro.

Big Mychael, carrying the pile of Little Mychael's birthday gifts, escorts us to our house. Mom answers the door, smiles very big at Mychael, hugs him, and slightly pats my head.

"Can we talk?" Big Mychael asks my mom.

"Sure," Mom replies.

As we enter the house, Big Mychael and Mom make their way into the kitchen. Big Mychael talks to my mom each time he takes us for the day. Sometimes, they talk for a long time, other times not. I think it depends on my mom's mood. If she's feeling good, the talk is long, but if she isn't, it's over quick. I have no clue what Big Mychael needs to talk to Mom about.

Whatever it is this time, it isn't much. Big Mychael leaves the kitchen and heads toward the door. He makes no eye contact with my brother or me.

"All right, boys," he says, as he walks out the door and gently closes it behind him.

CONVERSATION QUESTIONS:

Child: What are your thoughts on why one of your parents doesn't live with you? How do you feel when your father or mother leaves? Have you ever been left out? If so, how did it make you feel? What did you do when it happened to you?

Parent: Tell your child about a time you felt left out and what you did.

— Chapter 5 —

Sunday, Funday! (Ohmar)

On Sunday, like the typical family, we go to church. My mom and grandma see to it that we never, ever miss a day. I would be lying if I said missing Sunday football didn't bother me. It hurts like a paper cut. But Sundays are still fun.

At Sunday school, we get a chance to win small bags of soft mints, my favorite candy. Also, at church, I get to see my crush, Tina. Like me, she's in the fourth grade, but she attends school on the uppity South Side, so I only get to see her on Sundays.

Tina and I are the same height when she's not wearing her heeled church shoes. We're in the same Sunday school class, so I try my best to stand out and impress her. I'm the first to raise my hand to recite my Bible verse, and when I'm feeling more desperate to catch her eye, I recite a second verse that the teacher didn't even assign me.

It is the first Sunday of the month, which is Youth Day. That means the kids' choir sings, kids read the morning announcements, kids are the ushers, and those who win the Bible verse challenge get mentioned in front of the entire congregation. And what makes this day even more special is that all the kids who make the honor roll are taken out to eat after church.

I'm excited for all the opportunities to show Tina that I'm good enough to live on the uppity South Side and I am the boy of her dreams! At our church, the first step in getting attention is by dressing fresh. It's like a fashion show during the tithes and offerings portion when all the members stand up and place money into the collection plates while the choir sings. I might be ten years old, but I understand the seriousness of the moment, so I have to dress to impress—literally—to get that girl!

"Errrrr! This is too much pressure!"

"Boys, come get your church clothes!" Mom yells out from her bedroom.

My mom is a fashionista who usually spares no expense making sure Mychael and I look good on Sundays. She buys the finest suits money can buy. This time, she hands us matching light blue suits with navy blue clip-on bowties. Oh no! I hate blue! How could she do this to me, especially on such an important day as today? She has to have known that blue is not my favorite color. Does she hate me? And to make matters worse, I match my little brother! Tina won't take me seriously. And if she notices me at all, she'll think I'm the boy of her nightmares, not her dreams! Geez, my mom has really let me down this time. I think I'm going to have a panic attack!

Mychael sees the suits, gets very excited, and quickly snags his out of Mom's hand.

"Yes! It's like we're twins, big brother. I love it when we dress alike!" He gives Mom a big kiss on her left cheek and goes to put on his suit.

"Well, that makes one of us," I groan. "Mom, why do we have to wear the same suit? People are going to think we are twins when it's obvious we're not. I am three years older than him. Plus, blue isn't my favorite color. Why, Mom? Whyyyyy?"

"I had no idea you didn't like blue. You've worn blue plenty of times, including at school," she says calmly.

"Mom, red is the color I like now," I say.

"Well, I wasn't trying to make you look like twins, or to make you unhappy, Ohmar. I picked out the suits because I love the color on you and your brother. I want you both to know that you are handsome, and I love you equally. To make it easier, I picked out the same suit. I know that you and your brother have your own personalities, but I want you to be seen as equals for now. Plus, the price was right for me to get both suits. When you get older and get a job, you can buy your own clothes—and wash, dry, and iron them on your own too. And you know what happens when you get to that stage?"

"What's that, Mom?" I ask.

"You are going to be just as cute then as you are now," she says, gently pinching my cheeks.

"Oh, Mom!"

Church ends with no mishaps. I get recognized before the congregation for the Bible verse challenge, and Tina comes right up and says hi to me. Yes! I find out that blue is Tina's favorite color. Mom for the win again!

Mychael and I receive the invitation to attend supper with our pastor and the other honor roll students. For special occasions like today, we typically go to Nae's Kitchen restaurant, an all-you-can-eat buffet. I love it because I can try out all the foods I have never eaten before! I stack my plate with large, cheesy, thick-crust pizza (with anchovies) and pile it high with French fries! Mychael

chooses fried liver, fried okra, fried gizzard, fried chicken, fried apple pie, hot dogs, and beets!

The best part is that Tina sits next to me, and when it's time to get frozen yogurt for dessert, I press the button for Tina's vanilla and chocolate swirl cone. I think she might be the love of my life.

"Thanks, Ohmar," Tina says with a little grin on her face. As we leave, she looks at me bashfully and says, "See you next Sunday."

I want to say I think we "go together" now. Do we?

On the way to the car, I realize I've forgotten my football. I take it with me just about everywhere I go. I tell my mom to wait, so I can go back and get it. I rush into the building, grab it, and turn to go. Then, I'm surprised by a voice calling out from behind me.

I quickly turn around to see who it is, but I already know.

CONVERSATION QUESTIONS:

Child: In what ways does your mom or dad show you how much they love you? Is there a moment when you feel like you aren't loved and aren't special? What makes you feel loved or special?

Parent: Tell your child how you show them love and explain why. Explain what you do when you're not feeling "special."

— Chapter 6 —

Oh Dad (Ohmar)

"Dad!" I say excitedly. He gives me a great, big hug.

My dad is Vincent, a successful businessman. He's known around town as the go-to guy for all things electrical, especially for the wealthy people in the city. He is muscular like a professional football running back. I don't know why I don't see him as often as I see Big Mychael. My mom rarely talks about him, but my aunties tell me all about him—the good, the bad, and the ugly—most of the time without me ever asking.

I have this one auntie, my mom's little sister, named Sweetie. Yes, that is her name, and I will not dare question my grandma about why she named her that. Every single time I see her, Aunt Sweetie grabs my face and squeezes my cheeks, making me look like a blobfish. She looks deep into my eyes and tells me, "Boy, you look just like your daddy. Same smile, nose, mouth, eyes, hair, and walk."

Then, she says, "Your daddy is fine as wine."

She says I am going to be a heartbreaker when I grow up. I never really know what that means. What is a heartbreaker? What does a heartbreaker do for a living, I wonder? I assume it is a good thing, the way she says it. It sounds like a full-time job.

"Your mom tells me that you've been doing good in school," my dad says.

"Good? I've been doing great. Straight-As-great!" I say to him.

"Aw, man! I am so proud of you. Hold up! What are you doing with that football? Do you play a little bit?"

"Well, I play during recess every day at school. I am the fastest person in my class, next to a girl named Natalie. I heard she is so fast because she walks outdoors all summer long barefoot! Can that really happen?"

"Anything is possible…Hey, did you know that your old man was fast too, and was an All-Area quarterback in high school?"

"I didn't know that," I say.

"Yeah, man! We won the city championship in my junior year. How about I come to pick you up tomorrow after school to toss the old pigskin around? I can show you that I still got it. I hope you can catch a tight spiral," he says, winking.

I quickly nod my head. "Yes, I can."

My dad reaches into his pocket, pulls out his wallet, grabs a fresh, crisp two-dollar bill, and hands it to me.

"Don't spend it all on just candy and stuff," he says.

"Yes, sir…Also, is it okay for my brother Mychael to come with us too?"

"Yes, of course, he can."

Out of nowhere, some tall, slim guy about my dad's age walks toward him and gives him a firm handshake and hug.

"Vince, good to see you! Who do you have here?" he says. He seems surprised.

"Hey, Ron, my man. I want to introduce you to my son, Ohmar. You can call him Oh for short or Mr. Straight-A-Student," my dad says with pride.

Ron smiles very big, reaches out, and gives me a handshake.

Before I can utter a word, my dad continues, "Ron and I go way back to our days playing football in high school. We've known each other for many, many years now. I was the best man at his wedding a few years ago. Ron, now tell my son just how good I was on that football field."

"Oh, your dad was good, good!" Ron says. "In fact, he was unstoppable—the best quarterback who ever played at King High School." He looks at my dad. "Hey, it was really good seeing you up here. I'm going to call you during the week, so answer the phone."

"See, I told you so, son! I'm going to be there tomorrow to pick up you and your brother."

I walk away thrilled to have seen my dad, and that my brother and I will play catch with him after school tomorrow. But I'm somewhat confused.

Why did his friend seem so surprised when he met me? Did he not know I existed? There's so much about my dad that I don't know. Why did my dad introduce me to his friend as Oh? Only my family can call me that. I guess my dad needs to get to know me better too.

I soon realize my dad gave me two dollars. My mom taught my brother and me to always share, but with a solid two-dollar bill, I cannot give him a dollar.

I hurry back to the car, hop in, and say, "Mom, step on it! The candy store is calling my name."

"Candy store? You got money?" she asks.

"Yes, I do," I say as I reach into my pocket and pull out the two-dollar bill to show off.

Mom asks, "Where did you get that money from, mister?"

"My dad, for making the honor roll," I say.

"Oh geez...I want some money too," Mychael says.

"Don't worry, little brother. I got you taken care of. There is enough for the both of us."

CONVERSATION QUESTIONS:

Child: How would you feel if you were Ohmar in this situation? Has it ever happened to you that you felt like you were unseen or unheard?

Parent: What do you tell your friends about your child? What is something that your child may not know about you? Tell them why they are important to you.

— Chapter 7 —

Oh My, the Incident (Ohmar)

After we get home and put our things down, Mychael and I leave for Mattie May's Grocery Store to go candy shopping. Mattie May's is a small, family-owned neighborhood corner store. I've heard the family are immigrants who moved to the U.S. from a place unheard of to start their business.

Mattie May is a mean, short lady who speaks with such a thick accent that I can barely understand what she says. However, when it comes to money, I can understand her clearly. "Five dollars, one dollar. You don't have enough dollars," she'd say.

To be quite honest, where she and her family are from or how she talks is of no concern to me. Mattie May's has the best candy in the neighborhood—all kinds of candy. More than a kid could ever want. They even have candy from different countries. I can't read the labels, but it's very tasty.

Mychael and I are browsing down the aisles. I'm thinking about how I can stretch the money I have. I only have two dollars for both of us. Then, I have an idea—penny candy! I can get one hundred pieces for me and then give Mychael the change so he can get something for himself. After a few trips back and forth to the front counter, I have one hundred pieces of little sweet candies in a variety of flavors: cherry, orange, strawberry, apple, watermelon, fruit punch, lemon, and my favorite, grape! It's enough candy for me to eat for weeks!

At the counter, I am so proud of my new wealth. I pull out the crisp two-dollar bill, while Mattie May counts piece by piece, making sure that I don't have a piece of candy more than one hundred.

CONVERSATION QUESTIONS:

Child: What are you thankful for and why? How do you show your sibling or parent you love them? How do they show you that they love you?

Parent: Tell your child what you are thankful for and why. Explain what your relationship with your sibling(s) was like growing up and your fondest memory as a child.

STORE
50% off

— Chapter 8 —

My Store Experience (Mychael)

Being in this store with no money isn't a good feeling for me. Ohmar looks overjoyed as Mattie May counts the candy: "Fifty-one, fifty-two, fifty-three." I look up, and there it is…my favorite candy, Big Jon's Foot Long Saltwater Taffy. The price is $1.50. I won't have enough. Oh no! This is driving me crazy. I want this candy badly so I can bring it to school for my snack. All the kids in my class would ask for some, so I'd be the most popular kid in the class—well, at least for the day.

I wait for Ohmar to make his move to pay for the candy.

"Ninety-eight, ninety-nine, one hundred," says Miss Mattie May. I grab the Big Jon's Foot Long Saltwater Taffy. Ohmar hands over the crisp two-dollar bill. I tuck the taffy into my jacket.

Ohmar's Point of View

"Hey, you!" screams Mattie May.

Mychael looks up quickly, his eyes big as quarters, and runs out the door as if he is Speedy Gonzalez! I don't know what just happened. I grab my sack full of penny candy, forget my change, and run after him. I finally catch up to him.

"Boy, you are fast! What happened?"

"I took this," Mychael says with shame and pulls out a green apple-flavored Big Jon's Foot Long Saltwater Taffy from his pocket.

“Why did you take that?” I ask. “You’ve never taken anything that doesn’t belong to you in your life.”

“I just wanted my favorite candy, I guess. I wanted to be able to get what I wanted, but I didn’t have enough money. Big Jon’s Foot Long Saltwater Taffy is the favorite candy for all the kids in my class. If I bring it, they’ll ask me for some, and when I share, I will become popular like you,” Mychael says.

“Little bro, you’re already popular. You have tons of friends, and everyone likes you. You’re what they call an ‘A-lister’ in Hollywood. You don’t need to steal. How can we make this right…and fast, before the police come looking for the both of us?”

“Maybe I could return the candy and hope that Mattie May doesn’t tell the cops to lock me up and throw away the keys?”

“I like that idea of returning the candy,” I say.

Mychael and I return to Mattie May’s Grocery Store. As soon as we go in, we walk straight to the counter. Mychael is barely as tall as the counter. I imagine from her viewpoint, Mattie May can only see the top of his head.

“I’m so sorry. I took this,” he says quietly, putting the taffy in front of her. “Please don’t have guys in blue throw me in jail for life.”

Mattie May has no expression. In her thick accent she says, “Do not steal from me again! But…I appreciate your honesty. Most kids who take from me do not come back. Keep the candy.” She scoots the candy back to him with her knuckles.

CONVERSATION QUESTIONS:

Child: What is one thing you do that makes your sibling(s) smile? What do you like most about your sibling(s)? What do you like most about yourself? What is one thing you can do to make yourself happy?

Parent: Tell your child the one thing you like most about yourself and what you do to make yourself happy.

— Chapter 9 —

NeBo! (Ohmar)

On the way home from the store, Mychael and I are feeling pleased—until we spot the neighborhood stray dog, NeBo. He's humongous, old, mean, blackish-grayish, nasty, ugly, and dirty. He's been terrorizing the kids in the neighborhood for years. To this day, no one knows where this dog came from or who its owner is.

I remember one time things got so bad that we hung posters all around the town trying to find the owner, or someone to take this dog in, or at the very least, we thought the dog pound would take him. No such luck. And now…

"NeBo!" Mychael and I scream in unison and take off running like geese with one wing being chased by crocodiles! We run through alleys and race across the street, barely avoiding ongoing traffic multiple times, and so does NeBo. Cars stop at a screeching halt. No one is going to harm a dog, no matter how threatening he is! We hide behind trash cans but still cannot escape the ferocity of NeBo!

We run as fast as we possibly can, then I trip on the uneven sidewalk, fall, twist my ankle, and scrape my knee badly. Mychael turns around and screams.

"Mychael! Go!" I scream back.

Mychael's Point of View

"No, I won't leave you!" I shout. Then, I feel something hot on the back of my neck. I turn around. It's NeBo!

I look down, grab a stick, and try to distract NeBo but he just bites the stick and yanks it out of my hands. So I run as fast as my legs can go—toward a fence. Oh no! There's nowhere left for me to run!

NeBo is growling, showing me his enormous, sharp teeth. My chest is tight, and I can barely breathe, but I have to do something. I reach into my jacket and pull out the first thing I find.

NeBo jumps—it looks like a hundred feet in the air—as I pull out the Big Jon's Foot Long Saltwater Taffy (that I technically stole but then was given), hold it out in front of me and close my eyes. It feels like five hundred pounds of musty fur and bad breath knocks me over and lands on top of me. Sticky drool drips in my face as NeBo opens his gaping mouth.

He bites down on the giant stick of candy, tearing at it while it's still in my hand. He eats every bite, including the wrapping paper!

Then, NeBo starts licking my face. I start laughing as his large pink and black tongue tickles my nose, eyes, and forehead.

CONVERSATION QUESTIONS:

Child: What would you have done if you were in the situation that Ohmar and Mychael found themselves in with NeBo the dog? Was there ever a time you were scared and felt like you were in danger? If so, what happened?

Parent: Tell your child about a time you were scared and felt you were in danger. Explain what you did to feel safe.